Vocal / Piano

ORIGINAL KEYS FOR SINGERS

ISBN 978-1-4950-0238-0

HAL•LEONARD®
CORPORATION
7777 W. BLUEMOUND RD. P.O. BOX 13819 MILWAUKEE, WI 53213

Visit Hal Leonard Online at
www.halleonard.com

ALL SHOOK UP

Words and Music by OTIS BLACKWELL
and ELVIS PRESLEY

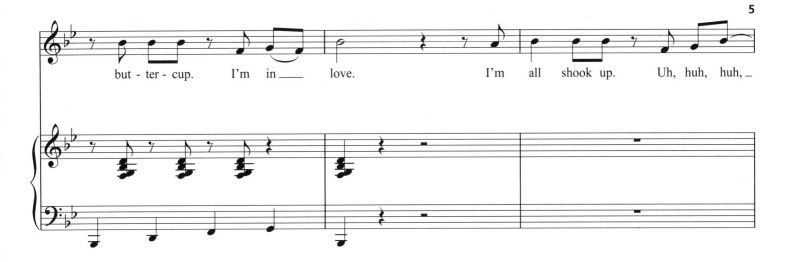

but - ter - cup. I'm in ___ love. I'm all shook up. Uh, huh, huh, ___

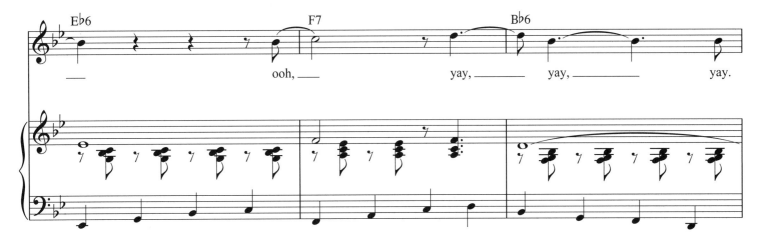

___ ooh, ___ yay, ___ yay, ___ yay.

My Uh, huh, huh, ___ ooh, ___

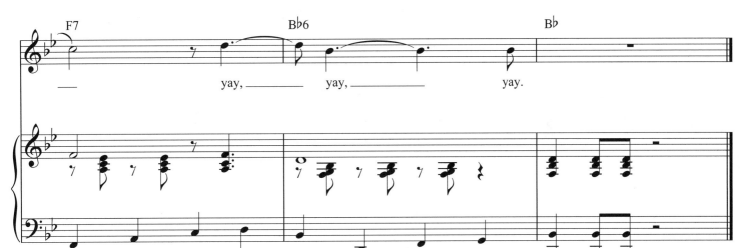

___ yay, ___ yay, ___ yay.

AN AMERICAN TRILOGY

Words and Music by
MICKEY NEWBURY

way, Dix - ie - land. ___ (Oh, I

wish I was in Dix - ie, a - way, a - way. In

Dix - ie - land I'll take my stand to live and die in Dix - ie.) ___

___ For Dix - ie - land, ___ that's where I ___ was born, ___

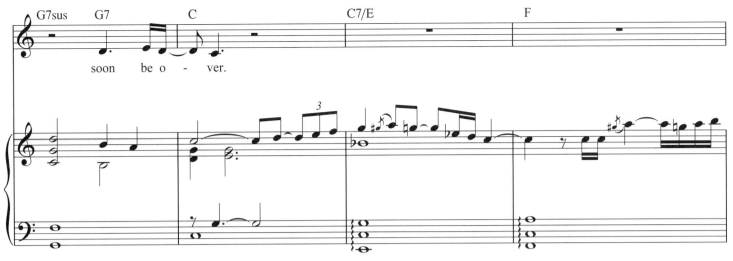

soon be o - ver.

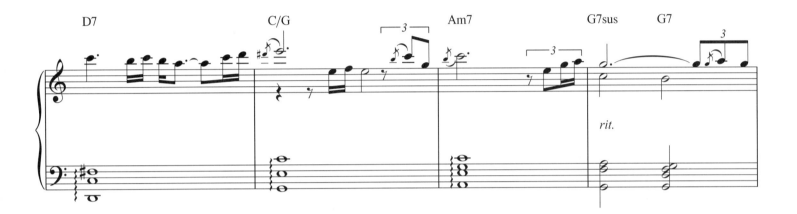

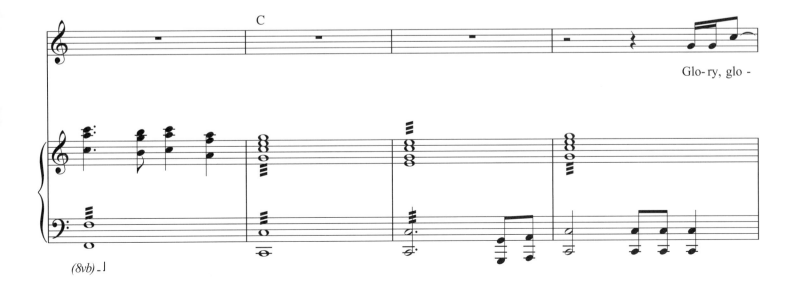

Glo-ry, glo -

(8vb) ⌐

-ry hal - le - lu - jah! His

truth is march - ing on. _____

_____ His truth is march - ing

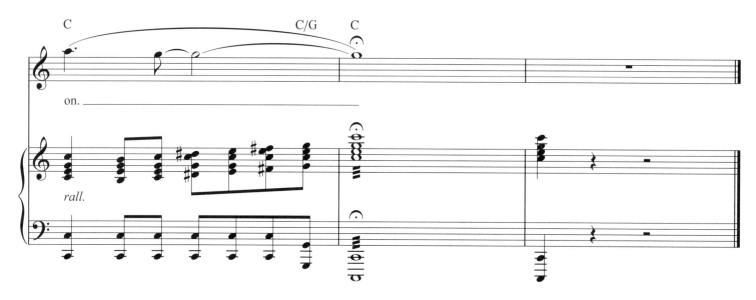

on. _____

rall.

ARE YOU LONESOME TONIGHT?

Words and Music by ROY TURK
and LOU HANDMAN

a cue.   *Then came Act Two. You seemed to change, you acted strange, and why, I've never known.*

Honey, you lied...   when you said you loved me,...   ...and I had no

cause to doubt you.   But I'd rather go on hearing your lies,   than to go on living

without you.   Now the stage is bare and I'm standing there   with... empti-

BURNING LOVE

Words and Music by
DENNIS LINDE

Lord a might - y, I feel my tem - p'ra-ture ris - - ing.

High - er, high - er,

it's burn-ing through _ to my soul. _____

Girl, girl, ___ girl, girl, you're gon-na set ___ me on fi-

-re. My brain is flam - ing;

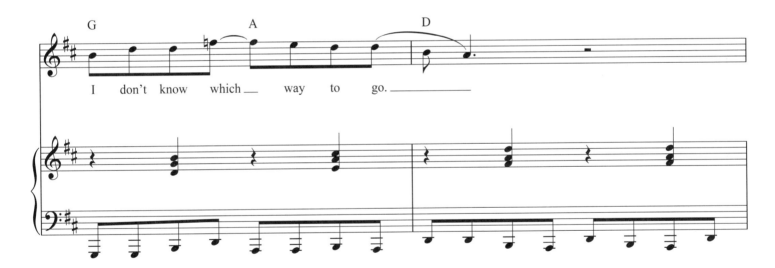

I don't know which ___ way to go. ___

Your kiss - es lift me high - er, like the

sweet song of a choir,_____ and you light my morn-ing sky_____

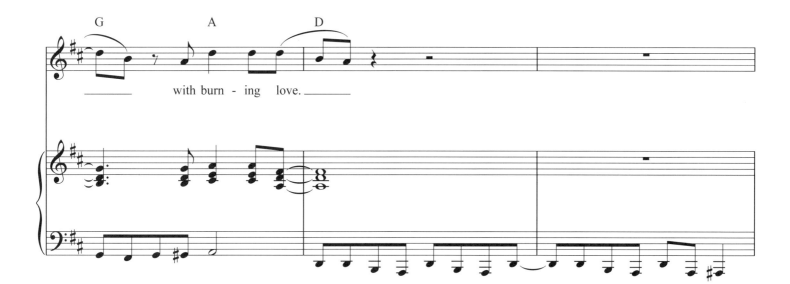

_____ with burn - ing love._____

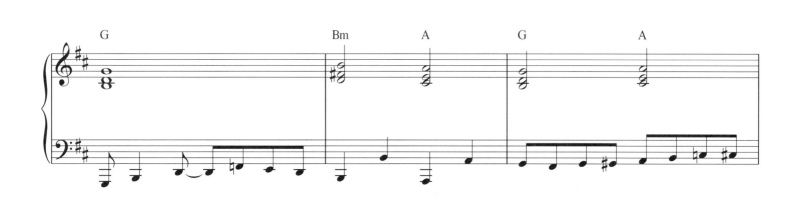

my chest __ is up-heav - ing.   Lord __

__ have mer - cy, I'm burn-ing a hole __ where I lay. __

__ Your kiss - es lift me high -

- er,   like the sweet song of a choir. _____   You

CRYIN' IN THE CHAPEL

Written by
ARTIE GLENN

CAN'T HELP FALLING IN LOVE

Words and Music by GEORGE DAVID WEISS,
HUGO PERETTI and LUIGI CREATORE

Moderately, in 2

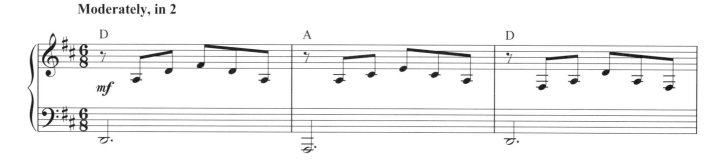

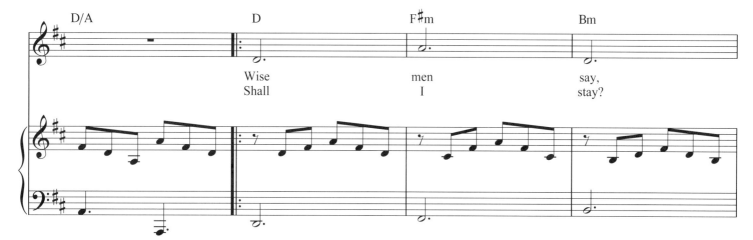

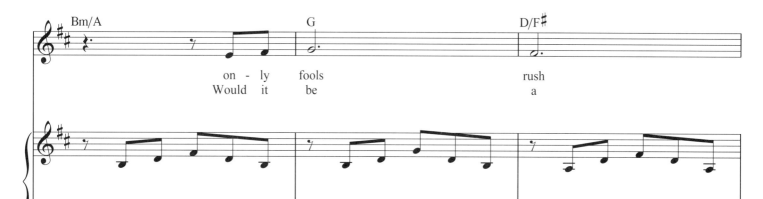

some things ___ are ___ meant to be.

Take my hand,

take my whole life, too.

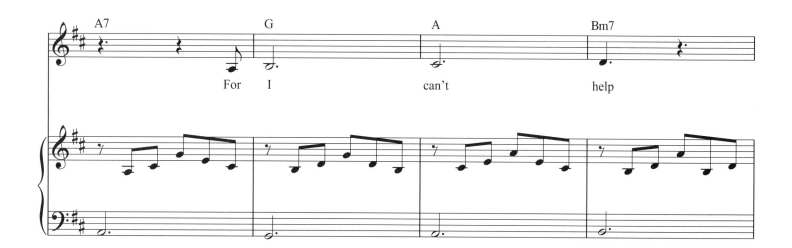

For I can't help

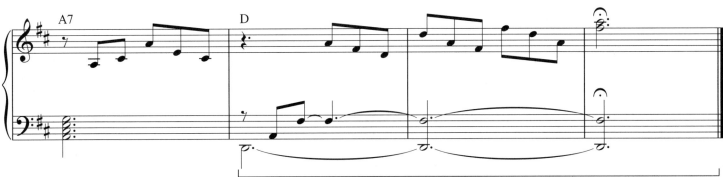

(You're The)
DEVIL IN DISGUISE

Words and Music by BILL GIANT,
BERNIE BAUM and FLORENCE KAYE

Tempo I

Heav - en knows ____ how   you lied   to   me. ____
Heav - en help ____ me: I   did - n't see ____

____ You're not   the   way   you ____
____ the dev - il   in   your ____

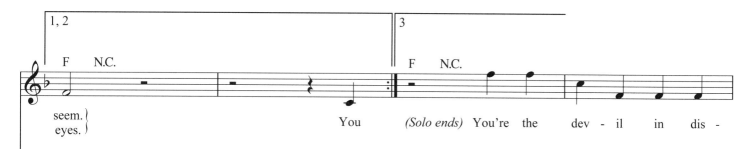

seem. }
eyes. }   You *(Solo ends)* You're the dev - il in dis -

guise,   oh, yes you are. ____   Dev - il in dis -

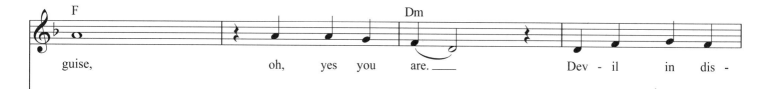

DON'T

Words and Music by JERRY LEIBER
and MIKE STOLLER

40

DON'T BE CRUEL
(To A Heart That's True)

Words and Music by OTIS BLACKWELL
and ELVIS PRESLEY

44

HEARTBREAK HOTEL

Words and Music by MAE BOREN AXTON,
TOMMY DURDEN and ELVIS PRESLEY

I'll be just so lone - ly, _____ I could die. Oh, al -
I'll be just so lone - ly, _____ I could die. Now, the
Well, they are so lone - ly _____ they could die. Well, now
You'll be _____ so lone - ly _____ you could

die.

Well, al-

though it's al - ways crowd - ed, well, you still can find __ some room for

bro - ken - heart - ed lov - ers __ to cry a - way their gloom. __ They'll be just so,

they'll be just so lone - ly, ba - by, well they're so lone - ly.

They'll be so lone - ly, __ they could die. __

(Now and Then There's)
A FOOL SUCH AS I

Words and Music by
BILL TRADER

Easy swing

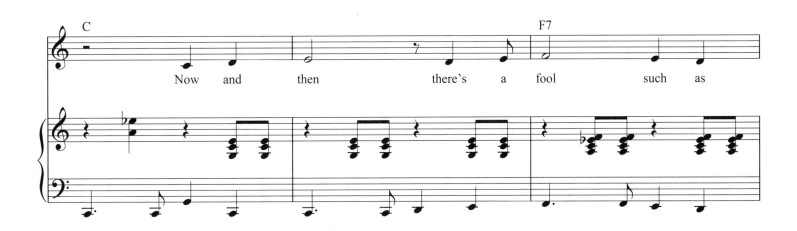

Now and then there's a fool such as

I. Par-don me _____ if I'm _____

_____ sen-ti-men-tal when we _____ say good-bye. _____ Don't be an-

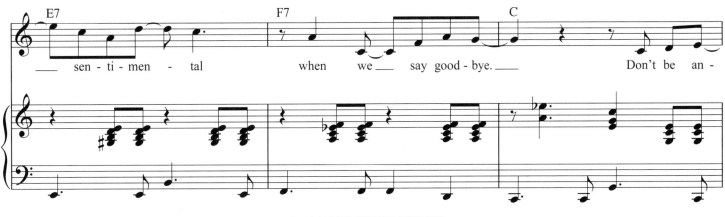

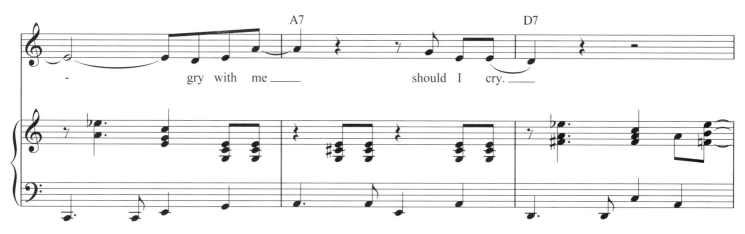

-gry with me _____ should I cry. _____

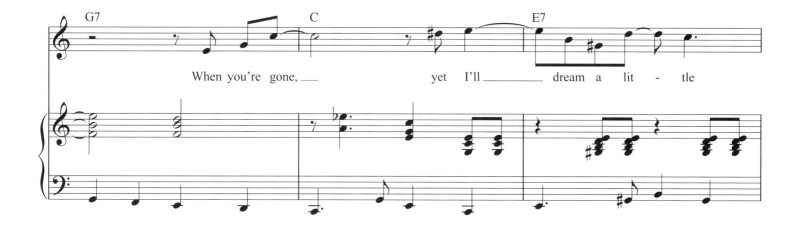

When you're gone, _____ yet I'll _____ dream a lit - tle

dream as _____ years go _____ by. Now and then _____ there's a fool _

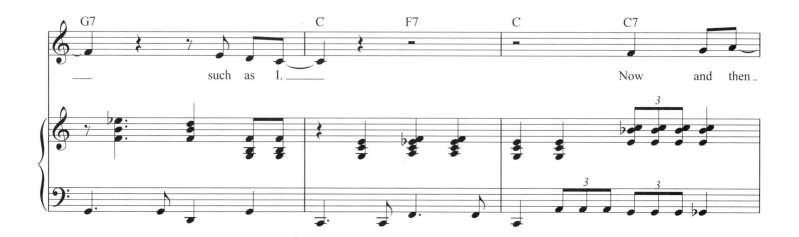

_____ such as I. _____ Now and then _

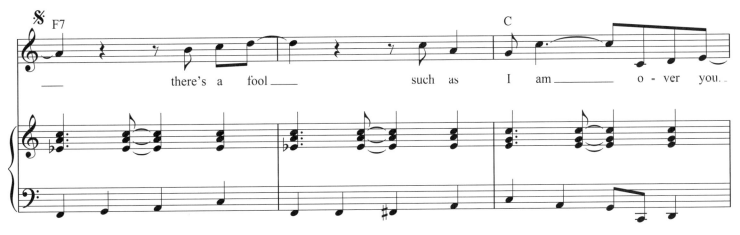

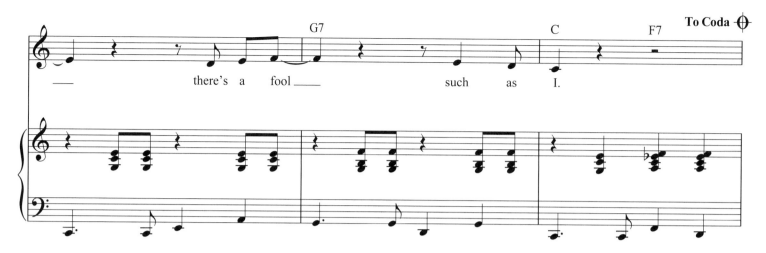

there's a fool ____ such as I.

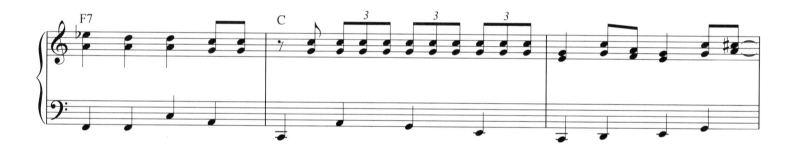

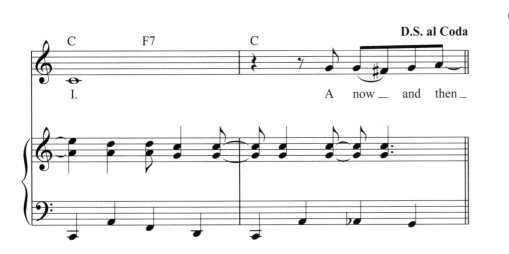

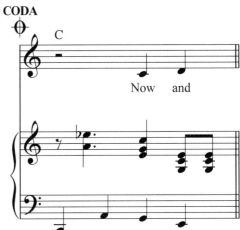

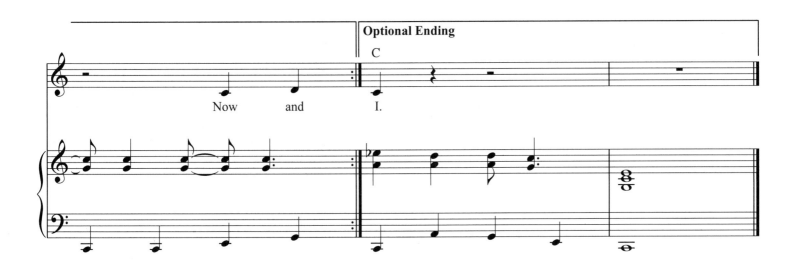

I NEED YOUR LOVE TONIGHT

Words and Music by SID WAYNE
and BIX REICHNER

Rock 'n' Roll

A oh, oh, I love you so.___ Uh,

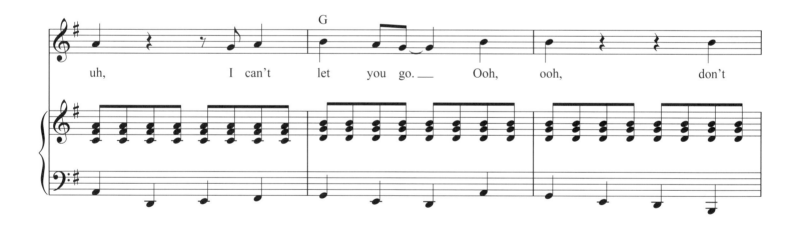

uh, I can't let you go.___ Ooh, ooh, don't

tell me no,___ I need your love to - night.___ Oh,___

tell me ba - by you've got to go. ___ I got the hi - fi high and the

lights down low. Hey, now, hear what I say. ___ Oh,

wow, you'd bet - ter stay. ___ Pow, wow, don't

To Coda ⊕

run a - way, ___ I need your love to - night. ___

I need your love to - night.

I

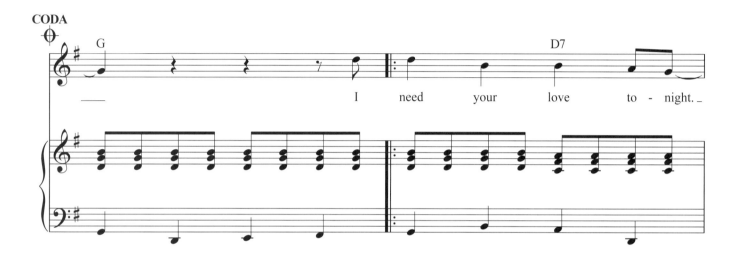

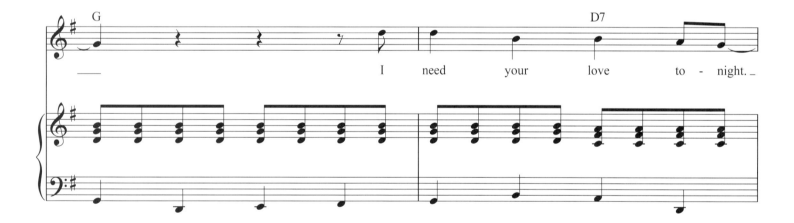

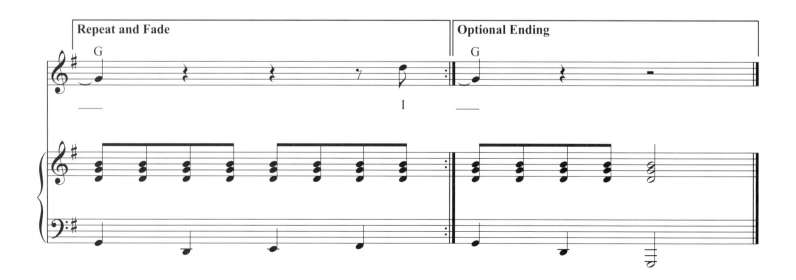

IT'S NOW OR NEVER

Words and Music by AARON SCHROEDER
and WALLY GOLD

Freely

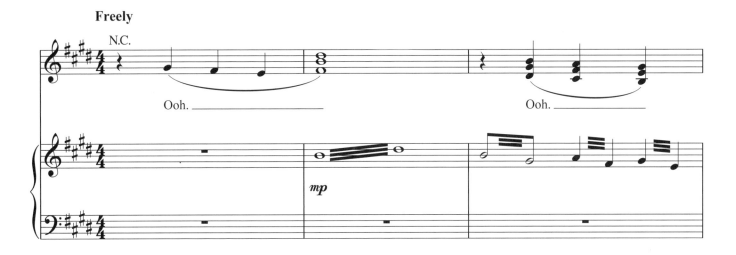

With a Rumba feel

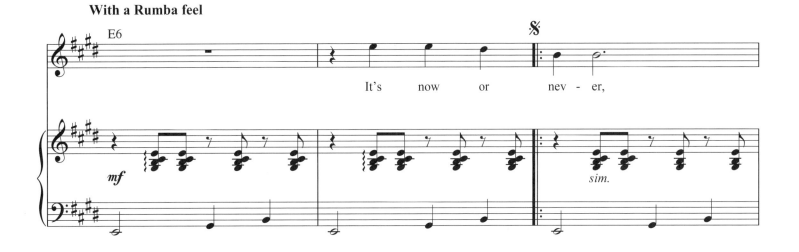

It's now or nev-er,

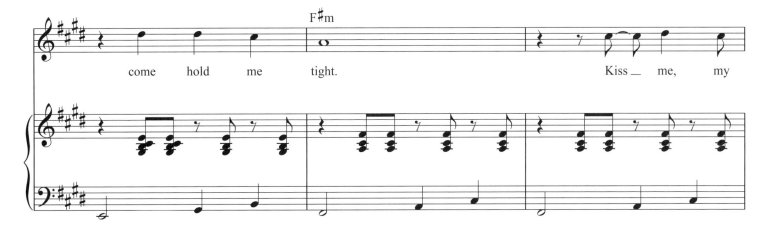

come hold me tight. Kiss __ me, my

dar - ling, be ___ mine to - night.

To - mor - row _____ will be

too late. ___ It's ___ now or ___ nev - er, ___

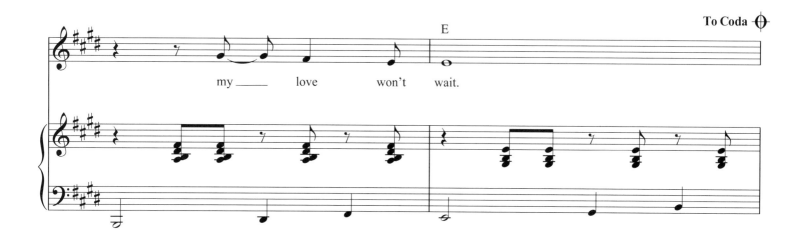

my ___ love won't wait.

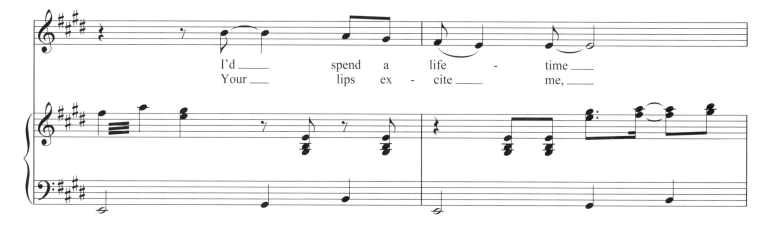

I'd ___ spend a life - time ___
Your ___ lips ex - cite ___ me, ___

wait - ing for the right time.
let your arms in - vite me.

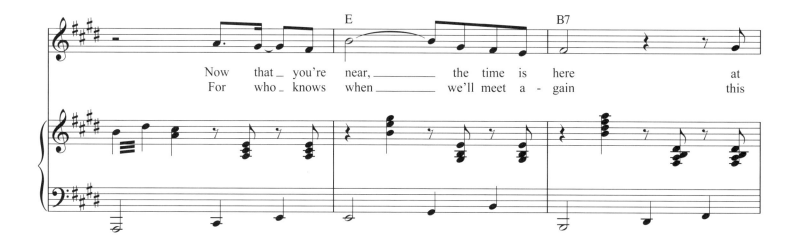

Now that _ you're near, ___ the time is here at
For who _ knows when ___ we'll meet a - gain this

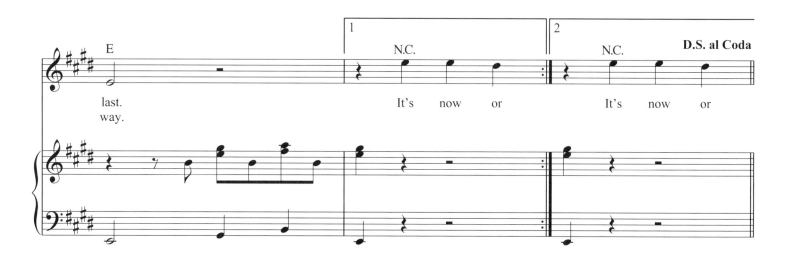

last.
way.

It's now or

It's now or

D.S. al Coda

CODA

It's __ now or ____ nev - er, ___ my __ love won't

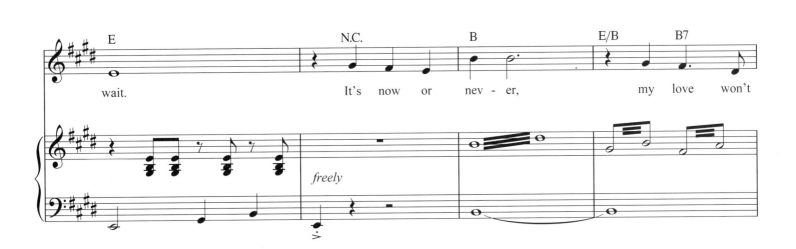

wait. It's now or nev - er, my love won't

wait. It's now or nev - er,

my love won't wait.

I WANT YOU, I NEED YOU, I LOVE YOU

Words and Music by MAURICE MYSELS
and IRA KOSLOFF

Moderate Waltz

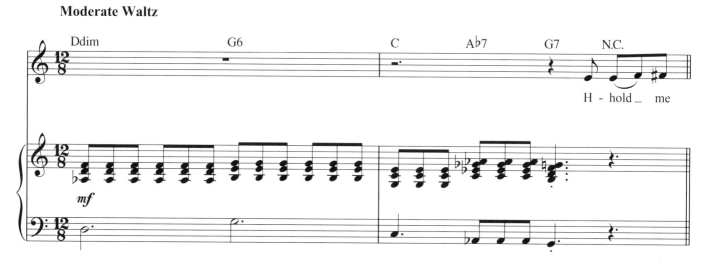

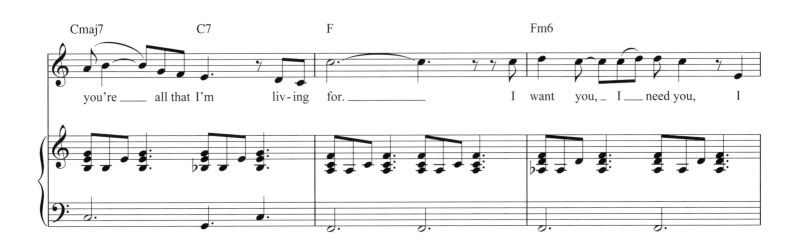

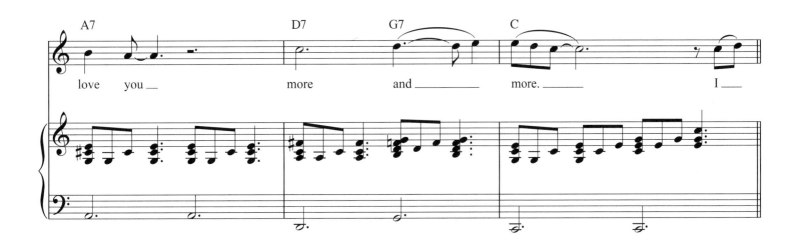

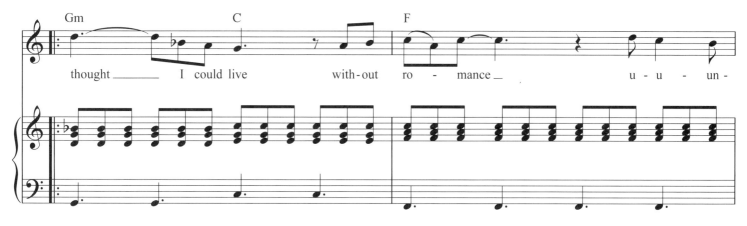

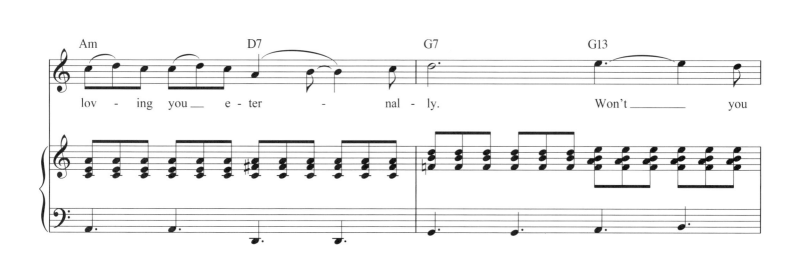

please _____ be my own, _____ nev-er leave me a-lone. 'Cause I

die _____ ev-'ry time we're a - part. _____ I want you, _ I _ need you, I _____

_ love you with all my

heart. _____ Well, I heart. _____

LOVING YOU

Words and Music by JERRY LEIBER
and MIKE STOLLER

A LITTLE LESS CONVERSATION

Words and Music by BILLY STRANGE
and SCOTT DAVIS

Rhythm & Blues

lit-tle less con-ver-sa - tion, a lit-tle more ac - tion.

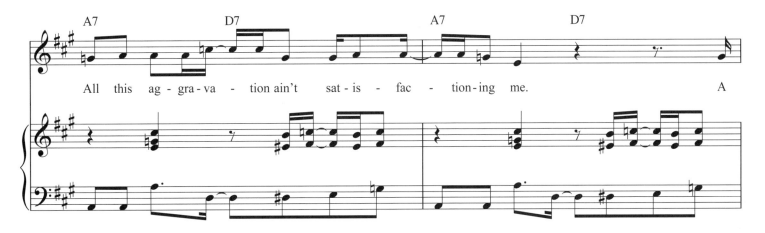

All this ag-gra-va - tion ain't sat-is - fac - tion-ing me.

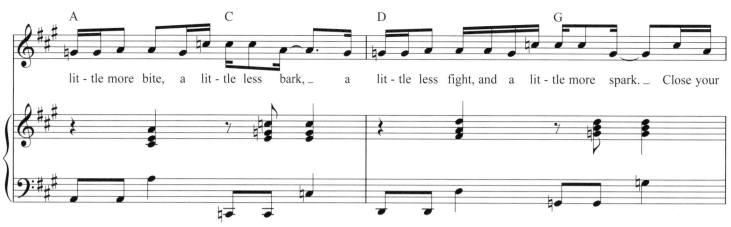

lit-tle more bite, a lit-tle less bark, _ a lit-tle less fight, and a lit-tle more spark. _ Close your

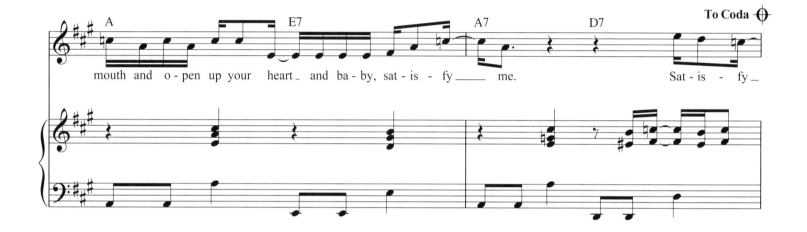

To Coda

mouth and o-pen up your heart _ and ba-by, sat-is - fy _____ me. Sat - is - fy _

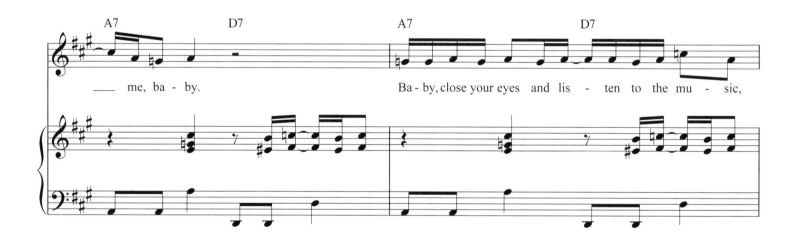

_____ me, ba - by. Ba - by, close your eyes and lis - ten to the mu - sic,

lean to the sum-mer breeze. _ It's a groov-y night and I can show you how to use it, now

come a-long with me and put your mind at ease, _ hey! A

_ me, ba-by.

Come on, ba-by, I'm ti-red of talk-ing.

Grab your coat and let's _ start walk-ing

Come on, come on. (Come on, _ come on.)

Come on, come on. (Come on, _ come on.)

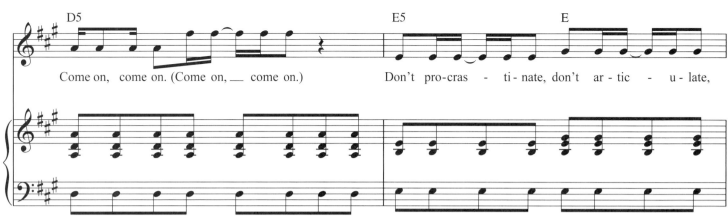

Come on, come on. (Come on, __ come on.) Don't pro-cras - ti - nate, don't ar - tic - u - late,

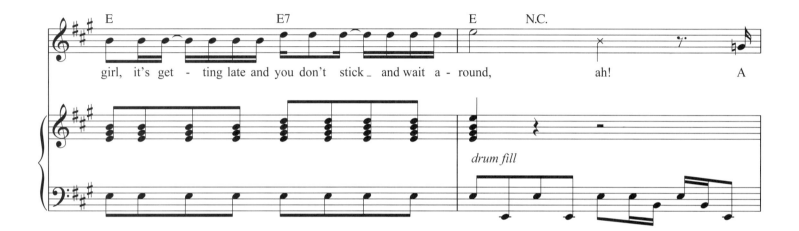

girl, it's get - ting late and you don't stick _ and wait a - round, ah! A

drum fill

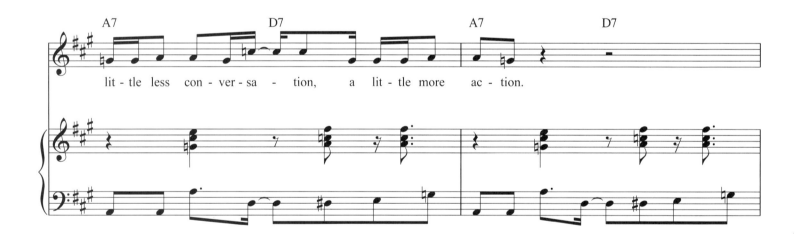

lit - tle less con - ver - sa - tion, a lit - tle more ac - tion.

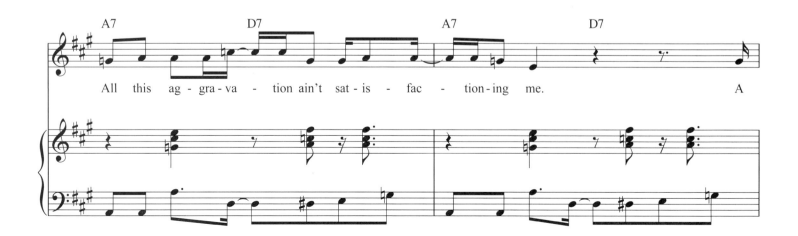

All this ag - gra - va - tion ain't sat - is - fac - tion-ing me. A

lit - tle more bit, a lit - tle less bark, _ a lit - tle less fight, and a lit - tle more spark. _ Close your

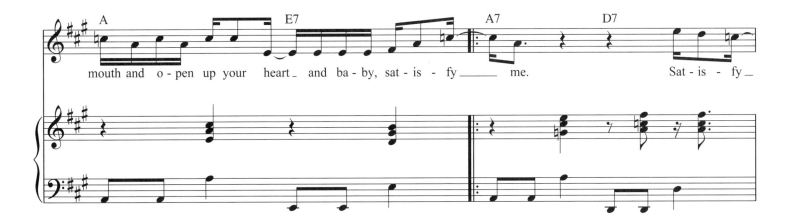

mouth and o - pen up your heart _ and ba - by, sat - is - fy _____ me. Sat - is - fy _

_ me, ba - by. Sat - is - fy _____ me. _____ Sat - is - fy _

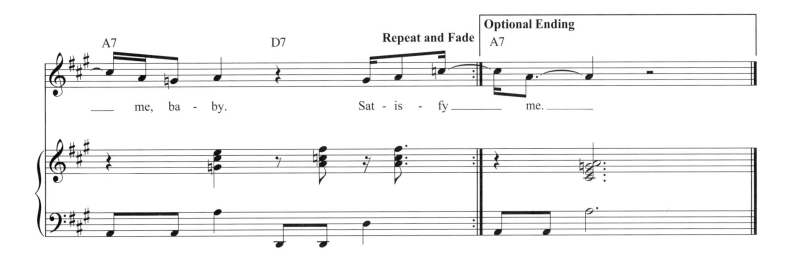

_ me, ba - by. Sat - is - fy _____ me. _

LITTLE SISTER

Words and Music by DOC POMUS
and MORT SHUMAN

Rock & Roll

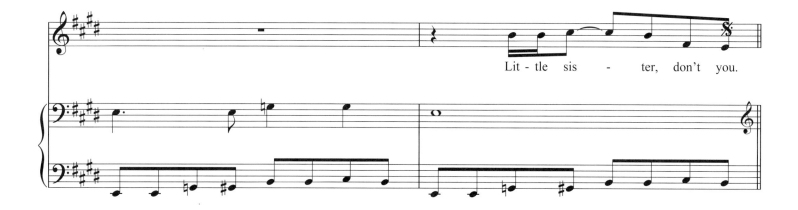

Lit - tle sis - ter, don't you.

Lit - tle sis - ter, don't you.

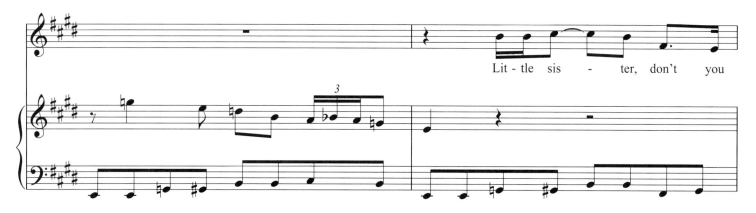

Lit - tle sis - ter, don't you

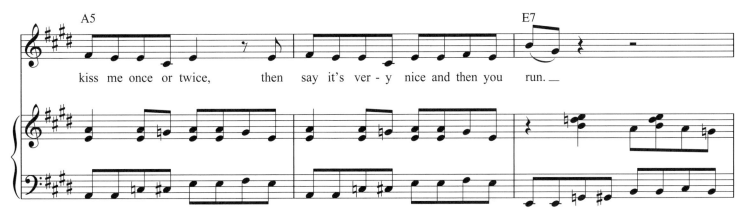

kiss me once or twice, then say it's ver-y nice and then you run. __

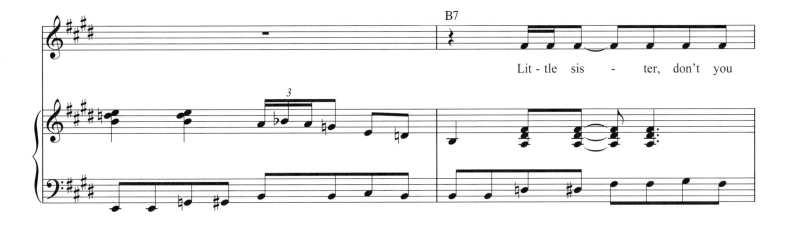

Lit - tle sis - ter, don't you

To Coda ⊕

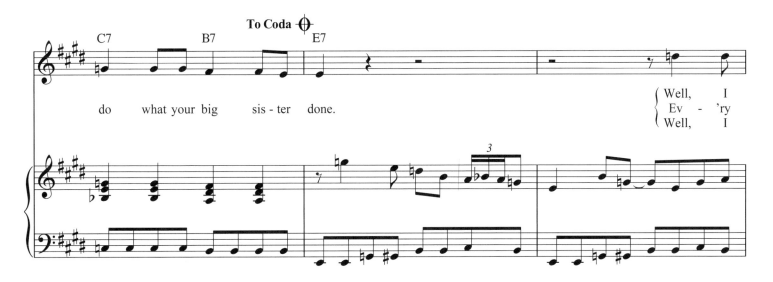

do what your big sis - ter done.

Well, I
Ev - 'ry
Well, I

dat - ed your big sis - ter and I
time I see your sis - ter, well, she's
used to pull your pig - tails and

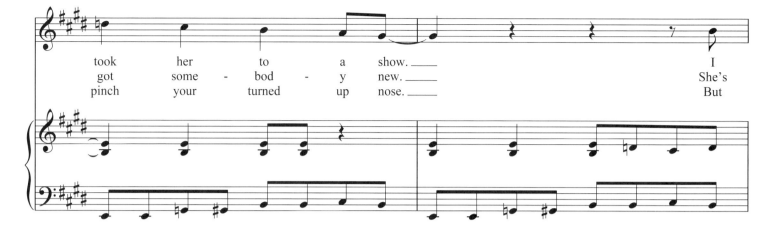

took her to a show. _____ I
got some - bod - y new. _____ She's
pinch your turned up nose. _____ But

went for some can - dy, a - long came _____ Jim Dan - dy and they
mean and she's e - vil like that lit - tle old Boll Wee - vil, guess I'll
you've been a grow - ing and ba - by, it's been show - ing from your

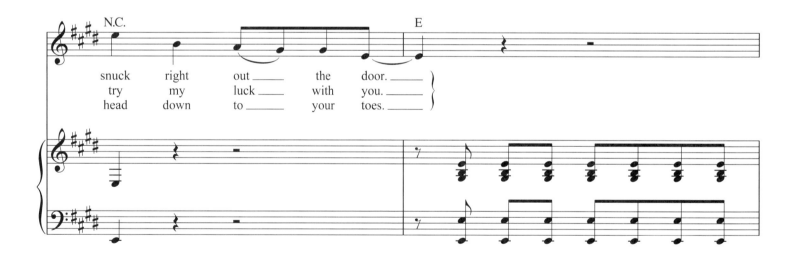

N.C.   E

snuck right out _____ the door. _____)
try my luck _____ with you. _____)
head down to _____ your toes. _____)

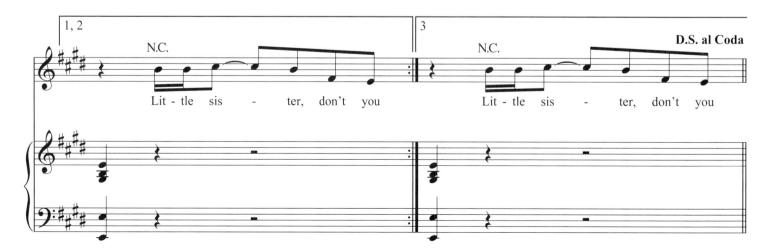

1, 2   3   **D.S. al Coda**
N.C.   N.C.

Lit - tle sis - ter, don't you   Lit - tle sis - ter, don't you

CODA

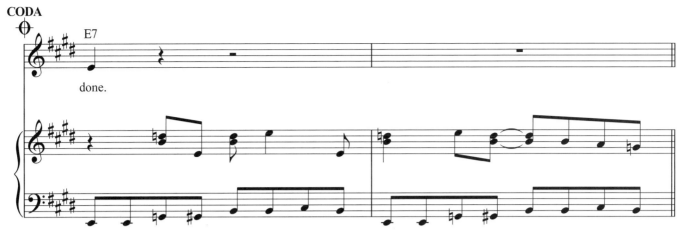

done.

Lit - tle sis - - ter, don't you do what your big sis - ter

Repeat and Fade

done.

Optional Ending

done.

LOVE ME

Words and Music by JERRY LEIBER
and MIKE STOLLER

Moderate Ballad

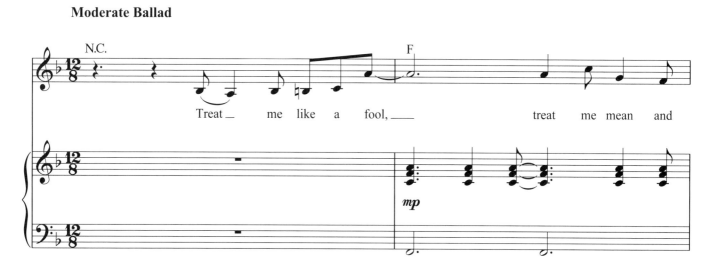

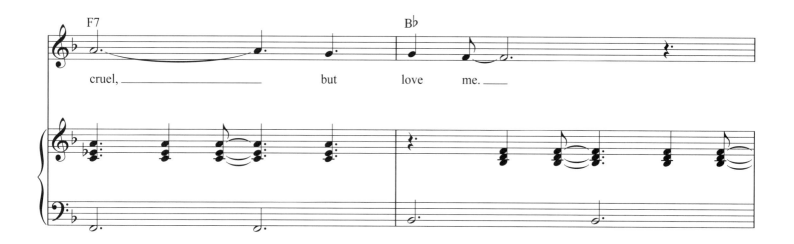

part, _____ but ____ love me. ____

(Won't you ____ love

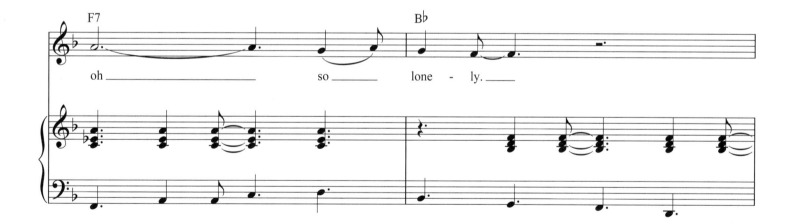

me?) Well, _____ if ____ you ev - er go, dar - ling, I'll be

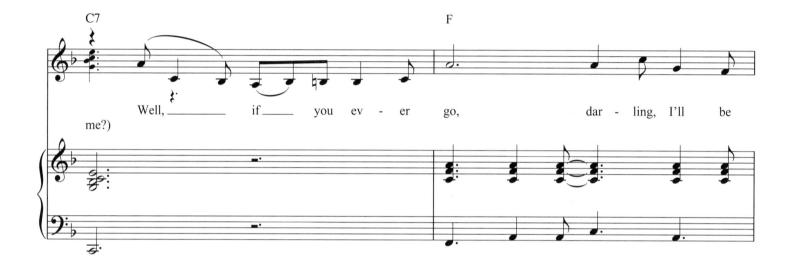

oh _____ so _____ lone - ly. ____

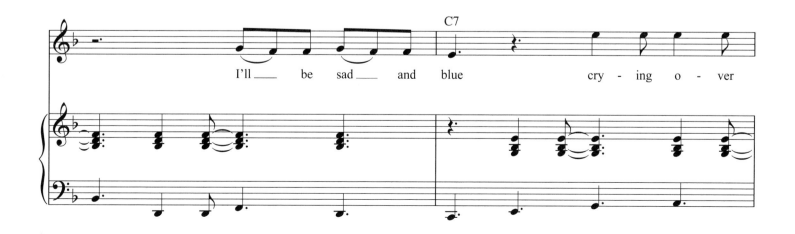

I'll ___ be sad ___ and blue cry - ing o - ver

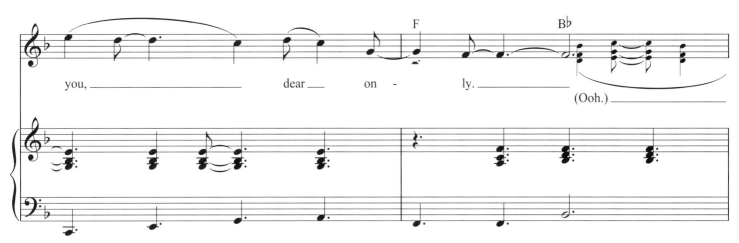

you, _____ dear ___ on - ly. _____
(Ooh.) _____

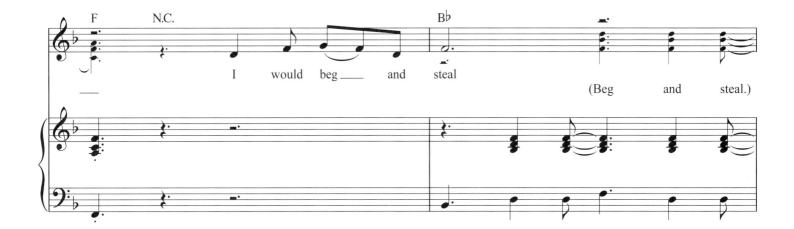

I would beg ___ and steal
(Beg and steal.)

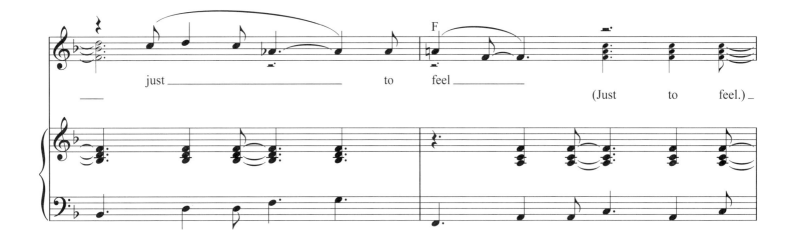

just _____ to feel _____
(Just to feel.) _

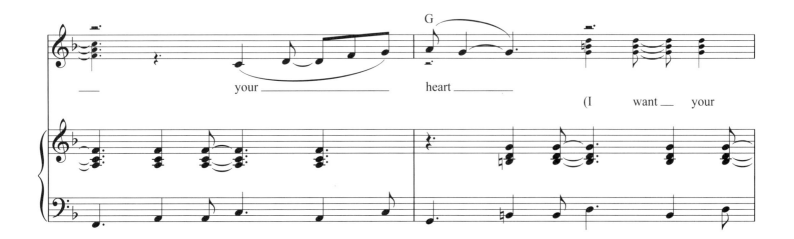

___ your _____ heart _____
(I want ___ your

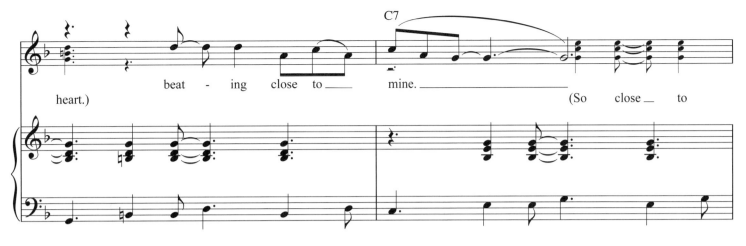

beat - ing close to ____ mine. _____ (So close ____ to
heart.)

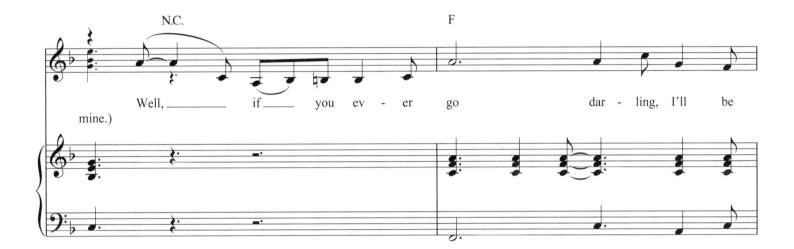

Well, _____ if ____ you ev - er go ____ dar - ling, I'll be
mine.)

oh _____ so _____ lone - ly. ____

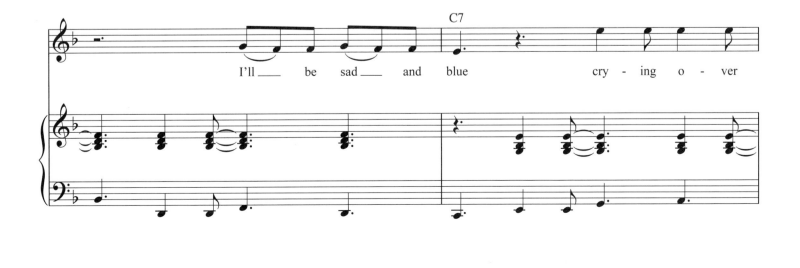

I'll ____ be sad ____ and blue ____ cry - ing o - ver

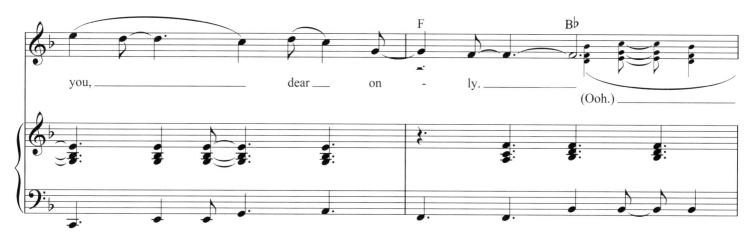

you, _____ dear ___ on - ly. _____
(Ooh.) _____

I ___ would beg ___ and steal
(He would beg and

steal.) just _____ to feel _____
(Yes, just ___ to

feel.) your _____ heart _____
(I want ___ your

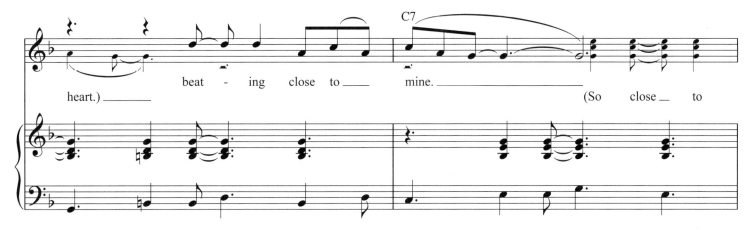

beat - ing close to ____ mine. _____ (So close ___ to
heart.) _____

Well, _____ if ___ you ev - er go dar - ling, I'll be oh _____ so ____
mine.)

lone - ly. ___ I'll ___ be sad ___ and blue cry - ing o - ver

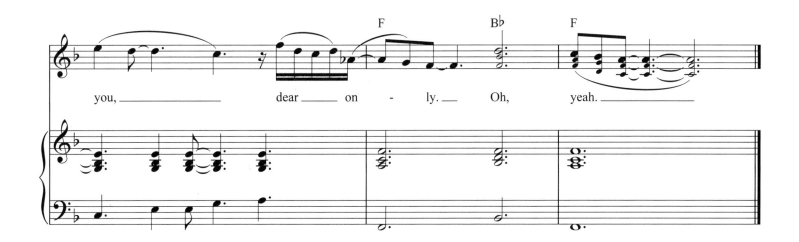

you, _____ dear _____ on - ly. ___ Oh, yeah. _____

LOVE ME TENDER

Words and Music by ELVIS PRESLEY
and VERA MATSON

Gentle Ballad

Love me _____ ten - der, love me sweet,
Love me _____ ten - der, love me long, _____
Love me _____ ten - der, love me dear, _____

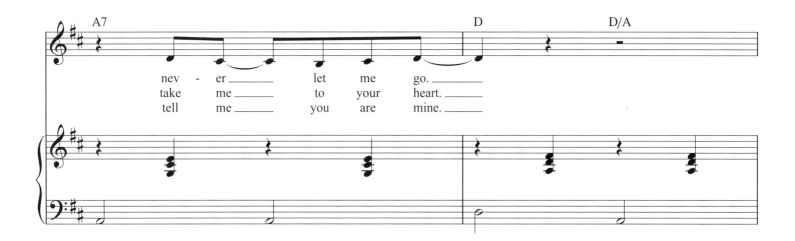

nev - er _____ let me go. _____
take me _____ to your heart. _____
tell me _____ you are mine. _____

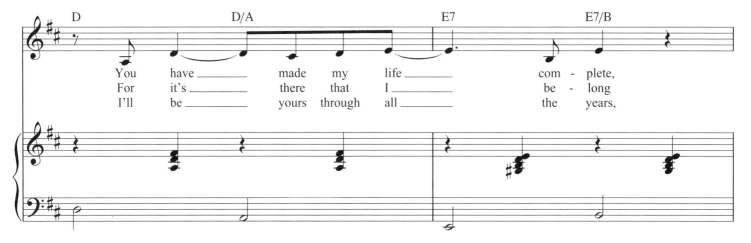

You have _____ made my life _____ com - plete,
For it's _____ there that I _____ be - long
I'll be _____ yours through all _____ the years,

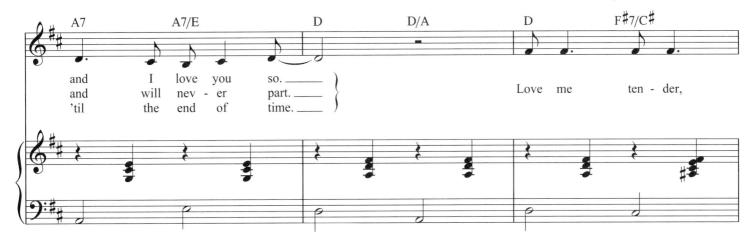

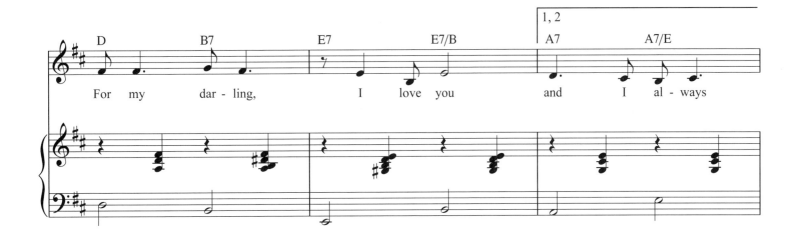

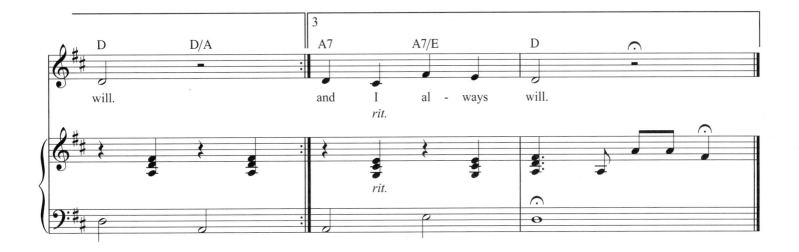

RETURN TO SENDER

Words and Music by OTIS BLACKWELL
and WINFIELD SCOTT

Re - turn ___ to send - er.

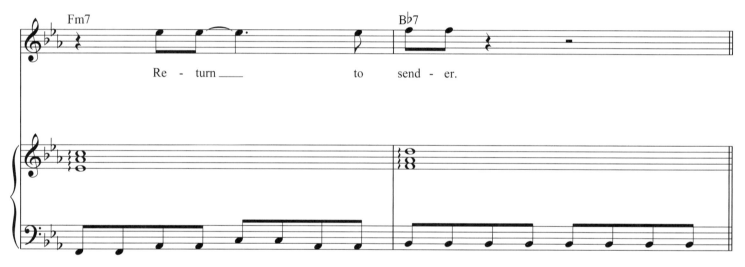

Re - turn ___ to send - er.

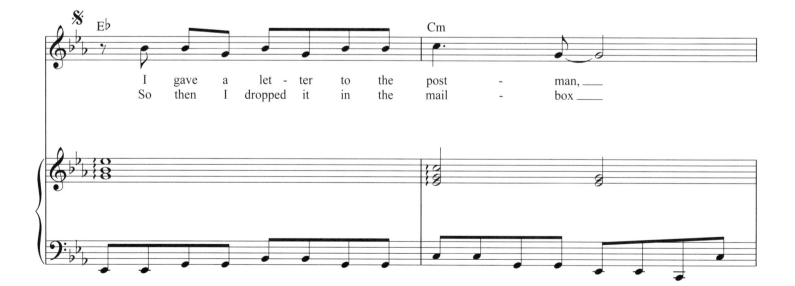

I gave a let - ter to the post - man, ___
So then I dropped it in the mail - box ___

he put it in his sack.
and sent it "Spe - cial D."
Bright and ear - ly next
Bright and ear - ly next

morn - - ing _____ he brought my let - ter
morn - - ing _____ it came right back to

back. }
me. }
(She wrote up - on it),
"Re - turn _____ to send - er.

Ad - dress un - known.
No such

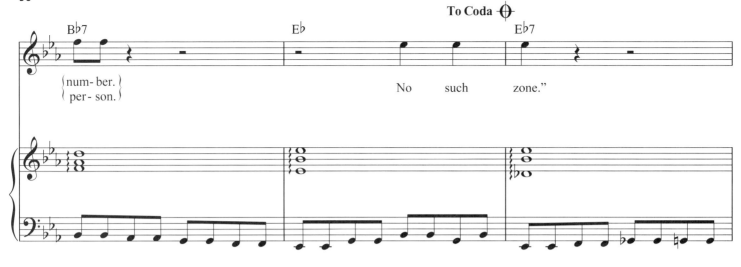

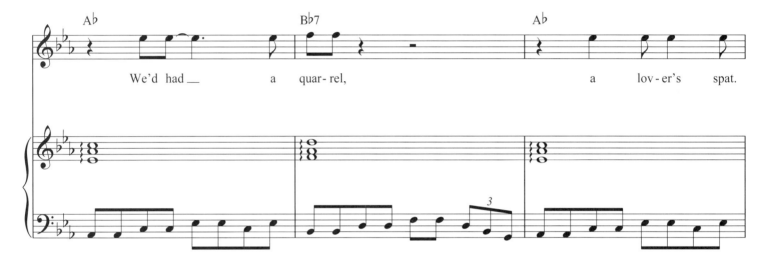

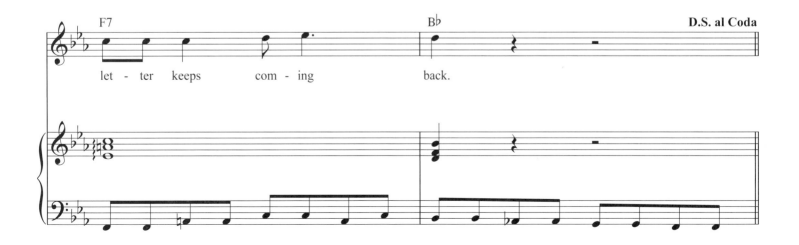

CODA

zone." This time ___ I'm gon - na take it my - self and put it right ___ in her hand, ___ and if it comes back the ver - y next day, ___ then I'll un - der - stand ___ (the writ - ing on it): "Re - turn ___ to

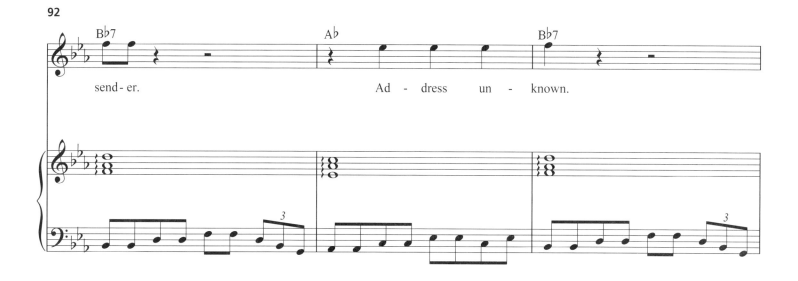

sen - der.

Ad - dress un - known.

No such num - ber.

No such

Repeat and Fade

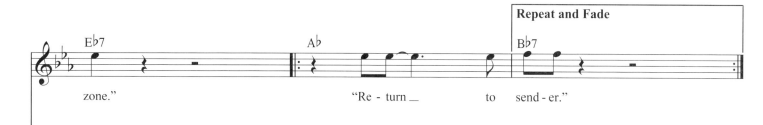

zone."

"Re - turn __ to sen - der."

Optional Ending

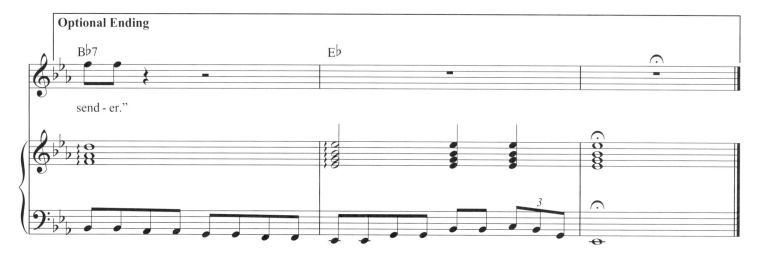

sen - der."

TOO MUCH

Words and Music by LEE ROSENBERG
and BERNARD WEINMAN

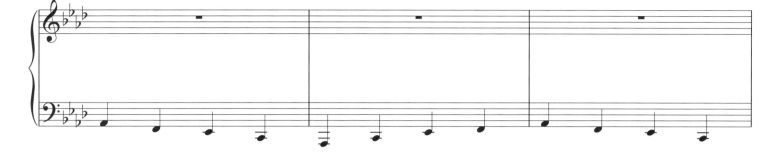

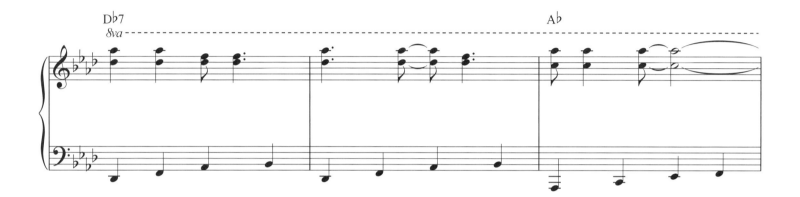

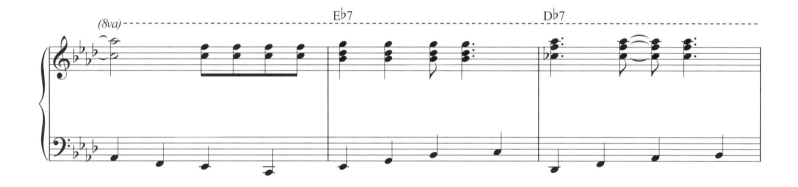

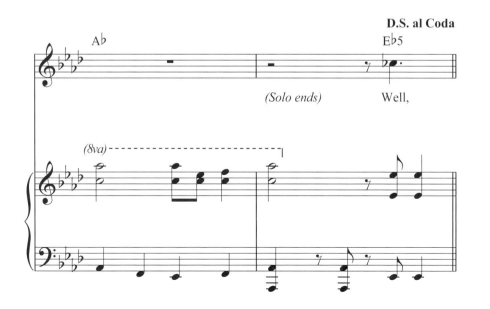

SUSPICIOUS MINDS

Words and Music by
FRANCIS ZAMBON

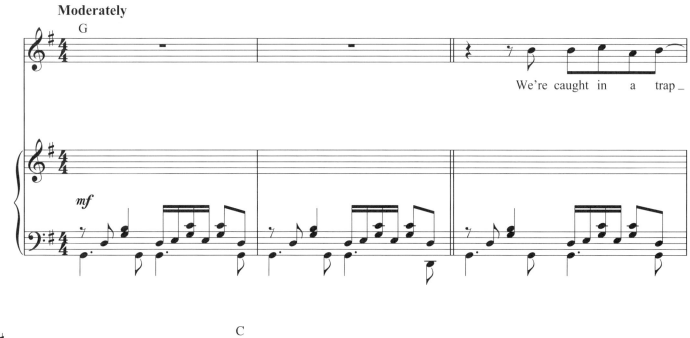

Why can't you see ____

what you're do - ing to me ____ when you don't be - lieve ____

____ a word ____ I'm say - ing? ____

We can't go on to - geth - er with sus - pi - cious ____ minds. ____

And we can't build our dreams on sus-pi-cious

minds. Won't let our love sur-vive

or drive the tears from your eyes.

Let's don't let a good thing die

Slowly, in 1

(Let Me Be Your)
TEDDY BEAR

Words and Music by KAL MANN
and BERNIE LOWE

you love e - nough.   I just wan - na

be   your _____ ted - dy bear. ___

Put a chain a - round my neck and

lead me an - y - where. Oh, let me be   your
                                                (Oh, let him be.)

THE WONDER OF YOU

Words and Music by
BAKER KNIGHT

Moderately, in 4

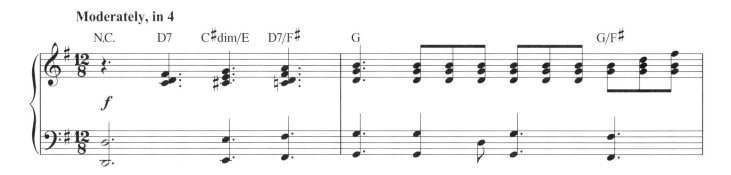

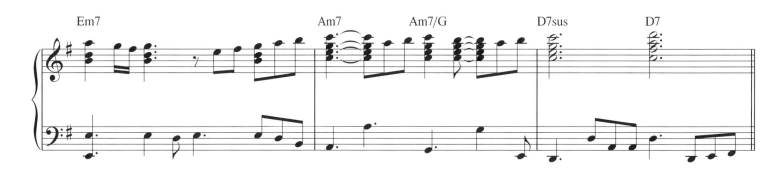

When no one else can un-der-stand me, when ev-'ry-thing I do is wrong,

the won - der ___ of you.

Ah, ah, ah,

ah. _____ Ah, ah, ah, ah. _____

Ah, ah, ah, ah. _____ I guess I'll

nev - er know the rea - son why ___ you

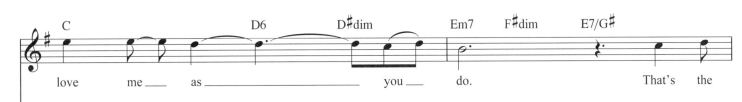

love me ___ as _____ you ___ do. That's the

won - der, ___ the won - der ___ of you. _____

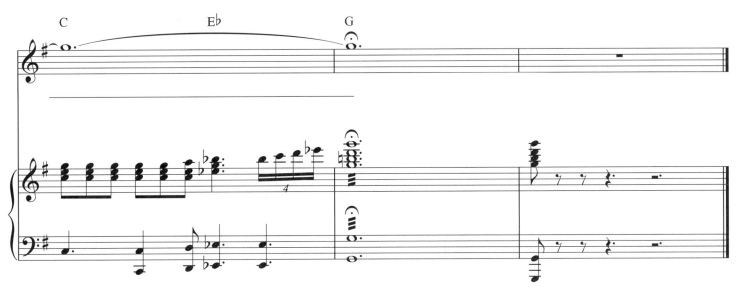

WEAR MY RING AROUND YOUR NECK

Words and Music by BERT CARROLL,
RUSSELL MOODY and MARILYN SCHACK

Won't you wear my

ring up a - round your neck

to tell the world ___ I'm yours, by heck.

____ to know the mean - ing of a ring. ____   I

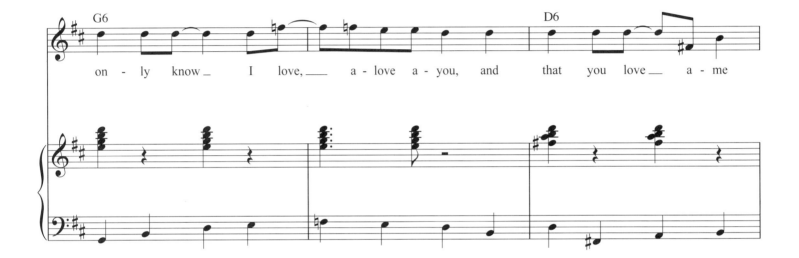

on - ly know __ I love, ___ a - love a - you, and   that you love __ a - me

too.   Oh dar - ling, this is   what I { ask ___ / beg ___ } of

you: Won't you wear my ring

120

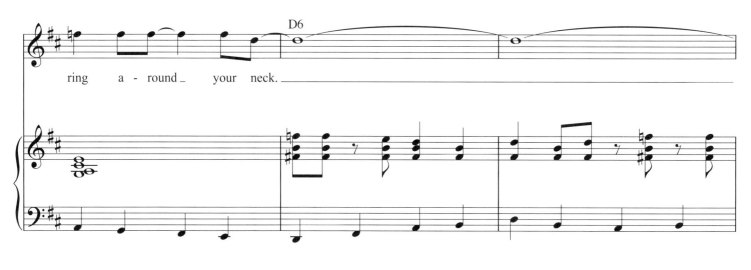